P9-EMK-141

FORENSIC FILES

INVESTIGATING
MURDER MYSTERIES

Heinemann Library
Chicago, Illinois

. . . PAUL DOWSWELL . . .

Originated by Ambassador Litho Ltd
Printed and bound in China by South China
Printing Company

08 07 06 05 04
10 9 8 7 6 5 4 3 2 1

**Library of Congress Cataloging-in-
Publication Data**
Dowswell, Paul.
    Investigating murder mysteries / Paul Dowswell.
        p. cm. -- (Forensic files)
Summary: Discusses some famous murder cases
and how forensic science
techniques were used to solve them.
Includes bibliographical references and index.
    ISBN 1-4034-4831-0 (Library Binding-
hardcover) -- ISBN 1-4034-5471-X
(Paperback)
    1. Murder investigation--Juvenile literature. 2.
Forensic
sciences--Juvenile literature. 3. Criminal
investigation--Juvenile
literature. [1. Murder--Case studies. 2. Forensic
sciences. 3. Criminal
investigation.] I. Title. II. Series.
    HV8079.H6D67 2003
    363.25'9523--dc22

                                            2003018157

Acknowledgments
The author and publisher are grateful to
the following for permission to reproduce
photographs:
p. 4 Science Photo Library; p. 7 National
Training Centre for Scientific Support to Crime
and Investigation; p. 9 PA Photos; pp. 10, 14,
19, 22 Corbis/Bettmann; p. 11 Science and
Society; pp. 12, 31 Dr. Jurgen Scriba/Science
Photo Library; p. 15 E.O. Hoppé/Corbis; p. 16
Robert Francis/South American Pictures; p. 18
Stephen Dalton/Science Photo Library; p. 20
Paul Smith/Panos; p. 21 Reuters/Popperfoto;
p. 25 Tek Image/Science Photo Library; p. 27
Neville Chadwick/Science Photo Library; p. 28
Frank Spooner; pp. 29, 32, 33, 34 Rex Features;
pp. 30, 35 Popperfoto; p. 37 Topham; p. 38
Doug Mills/AP; p. 40 Robert Sorbo/Reuters/
Popperfoto; p. 41 Susan Walsh/AP; p. 42
Philippe Plailly/Science Photo Library.

Cover photograph of a chalk outline
reproduced with permission of Aaron
Horowitz/Corbis.

Every effort has been made to contact copyright
holders of any material reproduced in this book.
Any omissions will be rectified in subsequent
printings if notice is given to the publisher.

Disclaimer
All Internet addresses (URLs) given in this
book were valid at the time of going to press.
However, due to the dynamic nature of the
Internet, some addresses may have changed, or
sites may have changed or ceased to exist since
publication. While the author and publisher
regret any inconvenience this may cause
readers, no responsibility for any such changes
can be accepted by either the author or the
publisher.

Some words appear in bold, **like
this.** You can find out what they
mean by looking in the glossary.

Contents

FORENSIC FILES

What Is Forensic Science?

Forensic science is any science used in a criminal **investigation.** Its purpose is to provide scientific **evidence** for use in a court of law. Forensic science draws on a number of different subjects, including chemistry, biology, geology, and computing.

A body lies face up, sprawled on the forest floor. It is that of a 30-year-old woman. Dressed in business clothes, she stares blankly up at the bright spring sky. A small bullet wound can be seen in the side of her head, and in her hand she clutches a pistol. An elderly man walking his dog comes across her and hurries to the local police station. "Looks like a **suicide,**" he tells them, shaking his head sadly. "What a thing to do."

Scene of the crime

The police officers have been through this **procedure** hundreds of times. Whenever a body is found in circumstances that suggest anything other than natural causes of death, the death must be carefully investigated.

First, a police officer rushes to the spot in the forest. His job is to "contain the scene"—that is, to make sure nothing around the body is disturbed. This includes preventing curious passers-by from adding their own footprints or fingerprints to the scene, possibly hiding vital evidence a murderer might have left behind. Then specialists called crime scene **investigators** arrive with detectives. Their job is to use their scientific and medical knowledge to establish exactly what happened.

This picture shows crime scene investigators at work during a murder investigation.

Searching for clues

The crime scene investigators are immediately suspicious—there is no blood around the head wound. Since the flow of blood in a person's veins and arteries stops at death, any wound that does not bleed must have been inflicted after death. This is definitely no suicide, although the body has been left to make it seem that way. The police warn the local **mortuary** to expect a new arrival. Another murder investigation has begun . . .

Crime scene procedure

Below are some of the procedures a crime scene investigator will follow when called to the site of a suspected murder:

- Record the scene: photographs, sketches, video footage, etc. all record in detail where the body has been found, and the position in which it lies.

- Establish time of death: a **pathologist** can estimate this, for example, by the temperature of the body. Body temperature is normally 98.6 °F (37 °C). After death, the body cools at a rate that can be calculated taking into account the size of the body and the temperature of the surrounding air. By working backward from the time the body is discovered, the approximate time of death can be found.

- Identify the victim: are there any documents to suggest who this is? If not, then a search of the police missing persons' **database** may reveal the identity of the deceased. Dental records, fingerprints, or **DNA samples** will also confirm a victim's identity.

- Collect evidence: anything around the body, such as a weapon, clothing, or fluid samples (blood stains on the ground that may have come from the murderer, for example) is carefully collected and sealed in airtight plastic bags.

Forensic Science in Action Today

First the body is taken to a police **mortuary,** and there a doctor known as a **pathologist** carries out an **autopsy.** A pathologist's job is to establish what killed a person and how it happened. Most importantly, he or she needs to gather medical **evidence** to help a court decide whether the death was a murder, a **suicide,** an accident, or the result of natural causes such as a heart attack.

Police lab

Specimens from an autopsy, such as blood or bullets, and any material taken from the scene of the crime, such as dirt from footprints, are then examined in more detail in a police laboratory. Today, **forensic investigators** use a whole arsenal of extraordinary machines to help them with their work. Computer **databases** sift through millions of files in seconds to match fingerprints and **DNA samples. Gas chromatography** can analyze small amounts of a suspicious substance and identify it. **Light microscopes** are extremely useful, although **electron microscopes,** which can magnify up to ten million times, are more suitable for examining minute samples of evidence. A machine called a secondary ion mass (SIM) spectrometer can analyze evidence that amounts to little more than a few atoms.

Looking for a result

When all this has been done, the police are presented with the results. They have material gathered from where the body was found, an autopsy report, and special police laboratory **data** gathered from high-tech **analysis.** All of this adds up to forensic evidence—scientific and medical facts that can then be used to work out the cause of death, solve a crime, and provide vital information for judge and jury in a murder trial.

Autopsy procedure

An autopsy, also known as a postmortem, conducted by a pathologist, is an essential feature of a murder **investigation.** A pathologist is a medical specialist who examines the tissues of a dead body to try to establish the how, why, and when of the death.

Clothing is removed, examined, and stored. Then the body is weighed, measured, and examined carefully for wounds or bruises, needle marks, rashes, or unusual color changes that might give some clue as to the cause of death. Hair samples are taken, fingernails are scraped for evidence, and samples of blood and other fluids that may be on the body are carefully removed and stored.

The body is opened up, and internal organs such as the brain, lungs, heart, and liver are removed, examined, and weighed. The organs may also be **dissected** and subjected to further tests in the police laboratory. The contents of the stomach and intestine are also removed for analysis. The organs are returned to the body (although some dissected samples may be retained), which is then sewn up and made to look as if no autopsy has taken place.

This scientist is at work in a forensic laboratory.

Forensics: the Early Days

Some of today's **forensic** techniques are based on those first used three or four thousand years ago in ancient Egypt. But it was in the mid–1800s that forensic murder **investigation** techniques took a form that would be recognizable today.

Dr. Edmund Locard, an 1800s pioneer of forensic investigation, famously reminded people working in forensics that "Every contact leaves a trace." That is, whenever a criminal touches anything, an object, a body, or even the ground, he or she leaves something there (skin **cells,** blood, clothing fibers, etc.) or picks up something from the scene that can be traced back. To this day, Locard's work is the basis of forensic scientific investigation and is known as **"two-way transfer."**

Forensic breakthroughs

During the 1800s five major advances changed the face of forensics.

1. <u>Microscopes:</u> invented in the 1500s, they could at first magnify only up to ten times. But by the 1880s improved **lens** design gave police scientists a microscope that could magnify up to 2,000 times. Stereoscopic microscopes, which provide a 3D image, and comparison microscopes, which allow two objects to be examined at the same time, are also invaluable. Now **evidence** too small for the human eye to see can be used to convict a murderer. All these microscopes use visible light, and are together known as **"light microscopes."**

2. <u>Chemical analysis:</u> the 1800s saw a huge leap forward in the understanding of chemicals. This was especially important in the detection of poisons such as arsenic, which had long been a favorite of murderers.

3. <u>Photography:</u> the first photographs were taken in 1827, and by the end of the century cameras were portable and reliable enough to be used for police work. By 1880, police arriving at a murder scene could record the scene with **glass plate negatives,** and refer back to an accurate photographic image when their investigations required it. In other words, they could produce a primitive type of photograph.

4. <u>Fingerprints:</u> the identification of criminals via fingerprints had become a standard practice by the 1900s. Edmund Locard advanced the technique significantly in 1918 when he introduced the idea of twelve matching points to be checked in fingerprint **analysis.** Prints discovered at a murder scene would often either lead to the murderer, or be used as evidence against him or her when other clues had led to an arrest.

5. <u>Ballistics:</u> the first criminal investigation to match a bullet to the weapon that fired it was in 1835. Today the science of **ballistics**—the study of projectiles (bullets) and the firearms from which they are shot—is a major part of police forensic work.

The Left-handed Lumberjack

On October 12, 1923, citizens of Portland, Oregon, woke to horrific news in their local paper. "FIENDS MURDER FOUR TRAINMEN IN COLD BLOOD" screamed the headline. The "fiends" in question were three brothers: twins Ray and Roy d'Autremont, and their younger brother Hugh, although the press and the police did not know this at the time. Just after noon on October 11 the men had carried out a carefully planned robbery on a train dubbed the "Gold Special." It would become known as "the Last Great Train Robbery"—echoing the lawless days of the Wild West, when trains were regularly robbed by outlaw gangs or reckless bandits.

Pictured here are the d'Autremont brothers, Hugh (left), Roy (center), and Ray (right).

Unlucky for some

The location of the crime was the neck of rail tunnel No. 13, south of Ashland, Portland, where trains slowed almost to a halt to test their brakes before the long ride down from the mountains to the coast. Here the Gold Special was hijacked by the d'Autremonts, who forced the driver to stop. Then explosives were attached to the locked door of the mail car, which they thought contained half a million dollars in gold, and a large sum of cash. Roy was responsible for setting the charge, and this was the d'Autremonts first big mistake. A far bigger charge than necessary blew the car to bits. Inside was mail clerk Elvyn E. Dougherty, who was killed in the explosion.

Victims two to four

The tunnels, acting as a huge sound amplifier, broadcast the bang over the surrounding area, and rail workers immediately began to race to the scene, thinking there had been an accident. The Gold Special's brakeman, Coyle Johnson, emerged amid the debris, smoke, and flames. He had walked up from the rear of the train to investigate. Startled by his sudden appearance, Ray and Hugh both opened fire with their guns, and Johnson fell down dead. By now the three brothers were confused, angry, and in a panic. They had killed two men and blown up the treasure they had hoped to steal. They killed the two other train staff who had **witnessed** their blunderings. Then they vanished.

Throwing light on details

Ever since **forensics** became a serious branch of criminal **investigations,** the ordinary **light microscope** has been one of the most important weapons in a forensic scientist's fight against crime. It was crucial in the d'Autremont case. Here is how a microscope works:

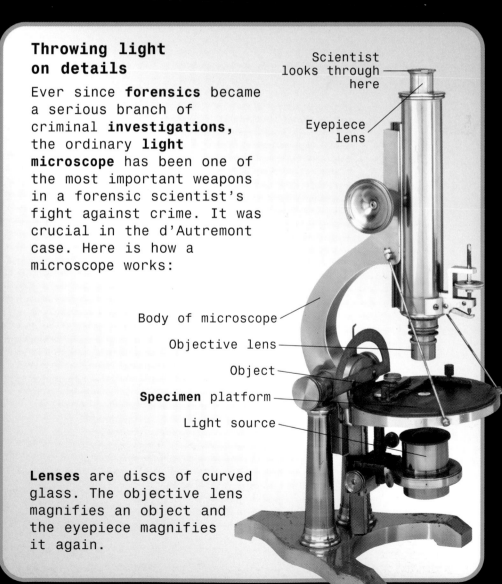

Scientist looks through here

Eyepiece lens

Body of microscope

Objective lens

Object

Specimen platform

Light source

Lenses are discs of curved glass. The objective lens magnifies an object and the eyepiece magnifies it again.

Looking for clues

When police and railroad workers reached the Gold Special and its murdered crew, they found several items the robbers had left as they fled. Among the items were a revolver, an explosive **detonator,** and a pair of overalls. With no obvious leads, the overalls were sent to **forensic** scientist Edward Heinrick, in Berkeley, California. From this one piece of clothing Heinrick was able to discover many details about its wearer.

Package giveaway

Heinrick found a receipt in a pocket of the overalls. Having been washed several times, the receipt could no longer be read. But when it was carefully unfolded, and treated with the chemical iodine, the details printed on it could faintly be seen. The trail led to Roy d'Autremont, whose neighbors admitted they had not seen him since the day of the robbery. The neighbors also agreed that Roy exactly fitted the description provided by Edward Heinrick. The police were sure they had their criminal. They obtained descriptions and photographs of Roy and his two brothers. Wanted posters were issued throughout the West Coast.

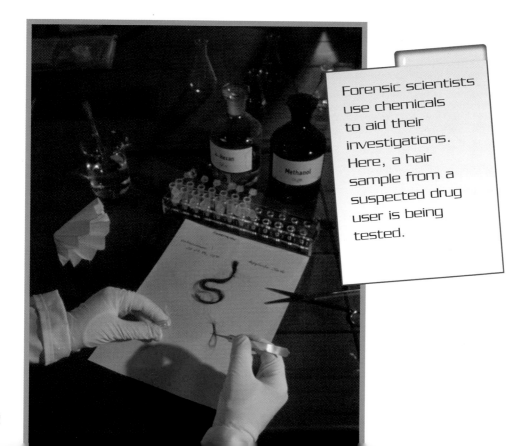

Forensic scientists use chemicals to aid their investigations. Here, a hair sample from a suspected drug user is being tested.

Justice is done

After the robbery the d'Autremonts laid low, and took on assumed names. Ray and Roy fled to Ohio, where they found work in the steel industry. Hugh joined the army and obtained a posting in the Philippines. But eventually people that knew the brothers recognized them from the wanted posters. When they were brought to trial, all three men were given life sentences. Roy suffered severe mental problems and was lobotomized, that is, forced to undergo an operation on his brain that was intended to make him very placid. He was never to be released. Hugh was let out in 1958, but died shortly after his release. Ray had his life sentence reduced in 1972. He died in 1984.

A life in pocket lint and fragments

Edward Heinrick described Roy d'Autremont like this:

Description	Clue
Height, 5'10" (1.75 meters)	approximate guess from size of overalls
Weight, 165 pounds (75 kilograms)	approximate guess from size of overalls
Hair, light brown	single strand found on overalls
left-handed	left-hand pocket of overalls used the most wear on buttonholes suggested buttons done up from left, rather than right
Habits, rolled own cigarettes	rolling-tobacco fragments found in pocket
neat and tidy	small nail clippings found in overall seam, suggesting a man who took care of his appearance
Occupation, lumberjack	pine tree resin and Douglas fir tree chips lodged in pockets

FILE CLOSED

The Bulgarian Umbrella Murder

FILE OPEN

On September 7, 1978, Georgi Markov stood waiting for a bus at Waterloo Bridge in England. Suddenly he felt a sharp pain in his right thigh. He turned to see a man with a rolled umbrella muttering an apology in a foreign accent. Then the man hailed a taxi and vanished. Soon after, a pimple-like swelling arose on Markov's leg. That evening he was taken to the hospital with a high fever. Doctors watched helplessly as their patient lapsed into a confused, excitable state, then died. Their verdict: ". . . blood poisoning caused by bacterial toxins (from microorganisms in the body) possibly a result of kidney failure."

Not so simple

Markov's death was suspicious. He had previously been forced to flee Bulgaria because of his work as a reporter critical of the **Communist regime.** He continued this work on British television. He had told his wife about the encounter with the man with an umbrella. It did not take a genius to guess that the previously healthy 49-year-old had been murdered.

Pinhead mystery

An **autopsy** was carried out on Markov's body. The pathologist suspected he had been deliberately poisoned, but could find no clear **evidence.** A section of skin around the pimple on his leg was removed and sent to a chemical warfare research laboratory. Scientists found a tiny metal ball the size of a pinhead.

Georgi Markov, the 49-year-old victim, was a Bulgarian immigrant.

The ball was sent on to Scotland Yard's **forensic** laboratory. It was examined by a scanning **electron microscope,** which uses an **electron** beam instead of light to view objects in extraordinarily great detail.

Gas gun killer

The police decided Markov had been killed by a gas gun (a gun powered by gas as well as gunpowder) concealed in the umbrella, which had driven the tiny ball into his leg. He had almost certainly been killed by a communist spy, on the orders of the Bulgarian leadership, which wanted to put an end to his criticism. The cause of death had been understood, but to this day the police have not tracked down the murderer.

Crime scene:
• Waterloo Bridge
• Victim attacked at 8:31 A.M. September 7, 1978.

Name that poison!

Forensic scientists skilled in toxicology (the science of poisons) assumed the substance that killed Markov was **ricin** for the following reasons:

• The dose was very small; only a few poisons, including ricin, are that powerful.

• The symptoms matched those of known ricin poison victims: weakness and fever, followed by internal bleeding and vomiting. Finally, the liver, spleen, and kidneys are likely to stop working, causing death.

• A pig, injected with a similar tiny dose of ricin, also died within 24 hours. Its internal organs showed the same damage seen in Markov's organs at his **autopsy.**

Guatemala's Killing Fields

They say there are two sides to every story, and this turned out to be the case for the villagers of Plan de Sanchez in Guatemala. Here, on July 18, 1982, in this Central American land of mountains and forests, a horrific **massacre** took place. On that Sunday morning 110 villagers—men, women, and children—were killed. About 60 survived by fleeing into the forest, and they **witnessed** the events from hiding-places. They claimed with great certainty that the killers were government soldiers. The soldiers **randomly** slaughtered whoever they could find. The government, on the other hand, claimed the villagers had been killed in crossfire, as soldiers fought left-wing **guerrilla** opponents of the president, General Efraín Ríos Montt. Some of the villagers were guerrillas too, they said, and had fired on the soldiers as they approached.

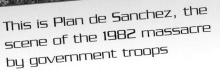

This is Plan de Sanchez, the scene of the 1982 massacre by government troops

Bad history

Guatemala is a very poor country, with a history of brutal dictators (cruel and powerful rulers). It was twelve years after these terrible events before the massacre at Plan de Sanchez was properly investigated in 1994. An international team of **investigators** arrived, under the direction of famed American pioneer of **forensic** anthropology, Clyde Snow. Snow, considered ahead of his time, has said "there is a brief but very useful . . . biography of an individual contained within the skeleton, if you know how to read it."

Talking bones
There are 206 bones in a human skeleton, plus around 32 teeth. Skeletons reveal a surprisingly large amount about their former owners.

Male or female?
The size of the pelvis is the best guide to the gender of a skeleton. Women have broader hips. Female skulls are usually smaller, smoother, and rounder than male ones, and their teeth are usually smaller.

Height
The obvious way to find the height of a person from their bones is to lay out the complete skeleton, and add on a small amount for the flesh of the heel. When a complete skeleton is not available, certain bones, such as the femur (thigh bone) or skull, give an idea of the height of a person. For example, the length of the head usually adds up to one eighth of the total body height.

Age
Age is the least reliable factor indicated by bones. With adults, the age of a skeleton can only be guessed within a ten year range. This is based on the wear of teeth, the rate infant **cartilage** has been replaced by mature bones, and the development of bone diseases such as arthritis.

On their own, each factor may not prove conclusive information regarding bones. There are, after all, tall women and short men. But taken together, the various factors usually add up to an almost certain identification of gender, height, and approximate age.

Sorting truth from fiction

At Plan de Sanchez, the team approached their job as if it was an archaeological excavation. Unlike a typical murder **investigation**, where crime scene **investigators** are presented with a freshly dead body and a host of clues, the team only had the testimony of village **witnesses** and several burial pits containing bodies that had been buried for twelve years.

Terrible tales

The first step Snow's team took was to interview village witnesses. Terrible tales were told by boys who had seen their sisters chopped to pieces, and there were harrowing memories of relatives burying women wearing necklaces they had given them on their wedding day. The government had flatly denied such testimony. If Snow's team could match the stories with hard **evidence**, it would prove the villagers had told the truth. Sure enough, female skeletons with arms separated from shoulders were soon recovered, and even skeletons with necklaces still around their bony necks. The number of women and children recovered soon laid to rest the story that this was a fight between soldiers and **guerrillas.** As the bodies were slowly revealed, they seemed to confirm exactly what witnesses claimed had happened.

Match that weapon

The claim that villagers were killed in crossfire was soundly disproved by examination of bullets and **cartridge cases** found among the burial pits and around the village. Cartridge cases carry an explosive that propels a bullet. As a bullet leaves a weapon along the barrel, the cartridge case is also thrown out at the side of the gun.

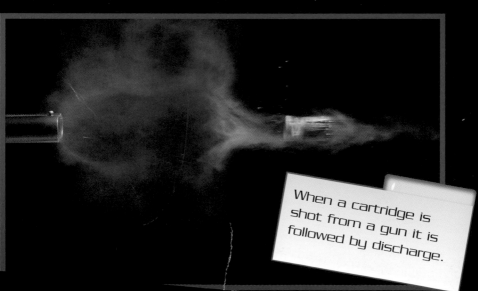

When a cartridge is shot from a gun it is followed by discharge.

Bullet

All bullets have small scratches (known as indentations) on them that give strong pointers to the type of weapon that fired them. All rifles have spiral grooves in their barrel, which make the bullet spin, and fly through the air more accurately. The spiral grooves leave distinctive marks that not only indicate the make of a gun, but can also pinpoint the actual weapon that fired the bullet.

The size of the bullet, known as its **caliber,** can also roughly indicate the type of weapon used.

Cartridge

The firing pin—the part of a gun that strikes the cartridge, triggering the explosive, which propels the bullet—leaves a distinctive mark on the cartridge, which indicates the type of weapon used. Also, all cartridges have a date of manufacture stamped on them.

All the bullets at Plan de Sanchez were 5.56 millimeters caliber. This matches the American M1 and M16 and Israeli Galil weapons issued to the Guatemalan army. The rebels used Soviet Kalashnikovs, which were 7.62 or 5.45 millimeters in caliber. No bullets or cartridges of this type were found in the village. This proved conclusively that there had been no battle between soldiers and guerrillas. When this became obvious General Montt changed his story, claiming that his predecessor ordered the killings. But all the recovered cartridges were manufactured in 1982— proof that the **massacre** happened in that year or later. Since Montt took power in March 1982, this further undermined his claim.

General Montt. shown here in center. speaks at a press conference.

The plot thickens

Over a period of twelve years underground, human tissue and clothing usually rot away, leaving only bones. But as the bodies of Plan de Sanchez were removed from the pits, the bones told a surprising number of stories. Excavating them was a very delicate task. Soil was removed a small layer at a time, and carefully examined for **evidence.** As bodies emerged, their positions were all meticulously noted. In a burial pit space translates into time. Bodies at the bottom had been thrown in first, and those at the top last. Careful recording of such details helps **investigators** recreate past events with greater accuracy.

Clyde Snow's team are shown at work in the killing fields of Plan de Sanchez.

Killing the evidence

During the **investigation** the members of Snow's team were threatened by strangers, and villagers and soldiers were told not to talk to them. Worst of all, Lieutenant Roberto Díaz, who had been in charge of the soldiers on the day of the **massacre,** was killed in his home by unknown gunmen.

Snow's team proved conclusively that General Montt's soldiers had carried out the massacre. There had been no **guerrillas,** and the event had probably been an unfair policy to wipe out likely supporters of the guerrillas—regardless of whether they were actively supporting them or not. But Montt was never brought to justice. As of 2004, he is still alive, and denies all accusations against him. He is too powerful a figure in Guatemalan politics to be removed. But, as Snow says, "It's hard to argue with a skull with a bullet in it, so this keeps (people) from coming along 20 or 30 . . . years later and saying 'These things didn't happen . . . .' Usually it's said that history is written by the winners. But with the help of science, history can be truth."

Whatever the present rulers of Guatemala may say, thanks to Clyde Snow and his courageous team, the rest of the world really knows what happened to the ill-fated people of Plan de Sanchez.

Tiny bones speak the loudest

One of the most horrific aspects of the massacre was that over a third of the victims were children. The skeletons of children reveal details about them much more clearly than those of adults. Children's bones can enable an investigator to estimate the age of a child's skeleton to within months rather than years:

- The size and height of a skeleton can give a good idea of a child's age.

- The teeth are a good indicator of age. Baby teeth are gradually replaced by adult teeth between the ages of seven and seventeen. Adult teeth usually come through at specific ages. For example, the adult front teeth generally emerge between the ages of seven and nine, whereas the rear wisdom teeth do not arrive until near adulthood, if at all.

- Bones of children are usually softer—still **cartilage** rather than hardened bone. The different bones of a skull are not fused together rigidly, as they are with adults.

The remains of some of the villagers killed at Plan de Sanchez are examined.

The Night Stalker's Simple Mistake

Richard Ramirez's neighbors regret the day he moved into their apartment building in Los Angeles, California. His long, thin face, with its bulging eyes and rotting teeth, did not invite conversation. He loved the rock group AC/DC, and would play their song "Night Prowler" over and over, sometimes for hours at a time. He took drugs too, especially cocaine.

Enter the Night Stalker

For three years, between 1983 and 1986, Ramirez terrorized the streets of Los Angeles and San Francisco. At first his **random** trail of killing, **assault,** and robbery was not noticed in the Californian papers. But when **evidence** gradually linked these crimes to one man, he became known as "the Night Stalker." Ramirez loved that name because it made him sound like a comic book villain. When he was arrested his tally of victims added up to at least 14 murders, 22 sexual assaults, and countless lesser crimes.

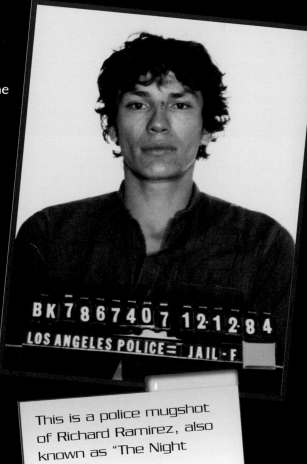

BK 7867407 121284
LOS ANGELES POLICE JAIL-F

This is a police mugshot of Richard Ramirez, also known as "The Night Stalker."

A simple catch

Ramirez was caught because of some basic errors. In March 1985 one victim provided police with a good description. Five months later, another victim noted the license plate on his car as he sped away from an assault that left her badly injured but still alive. It was a stolen car, but police traced the vehicle and found a fingerprint. They matched the fingerprint to one already on file, taken from Ramirez when he had committed a burglary in the early 1980s. On August 31, the Night Stalker found his own face staring out at him from every newspaper in town. He was set upon by an angry mob, and escaped a lynching (being killed by a mob) only when a police officer arrested him. Further evidence, such as footprint samples and firearm matches (Ramirez did not throw away the guns he used to shoot his victims), proved conclusively that the police had their man.

Death sentence

During his trial Ramirez showed no remorse, or sign of regret. Reveling in his bad reputation, he waved to press photographers, and shouted "Hail Satan." The judge was unimpressed, and sent him to a prison block for prisoners sentenced to death. As of 2004, Ramirez is still there awaiting execution.

Fingerprint file

The simple fingerprint, one of the earliest tools of **forensic investigators,** is still immensely useful. Forensic teams around the world rely on a complicated system of filing and comparing prints from police **databases.** Computer programs have sped up the process of identifying fingerprints. The basic technique is still similar to the process established by Czech physiologist Johannes Evangelista Purkyně in 1823. Although everyone has their own unique set of fingerprints, there are four basic types: loop, arch, whorl, and accidental.

Fingerprints show up on glass, dirt, and especially in bloody handprints. Often though, prints on tables, light switches, or other surfaces can only be seen when dusted with a special powder.

The Pitchfork Murders

In 1983 the body of fifteen-year-old Lynda Mann was discovered on a secluded Narborough, England, footpath one bleak fall morning. Police called to the scene quickly discovered she had been attacked and strangled. **Evidence** was slim—there was some **forensic** traces from the killer and a suspicion that they were looking for a local man. After all, only local people would know about the footpath where she was found. A psychiatric hospital in the area became the focus of the **investigation.** One man, who had a number of convictions for harassing local women, was a prime suspect. But forensic tests showed he was not the murderer.

Same again

Time passed, and the police had to admit their investigation had drawn a blank. Then, in summer 1986, an almost identical murder occurred. The victim, Dawn Ashworth, also fifteen years old, was found less than a mile away from the spot where Lynda Mann's body was found. This time, a suspect quickly turned up. A local hospital worker had talked about the crime with colleagues the night before the news broke, and the police were quickly alerted. The suspect was a seventeen-year-old of low intelligence, who drove a motorcycle and wore a red crash helmet. Other leads revealed that a motorcyclist with a red crash helmet had been seen near where Ashworth's body had been found. The boy readily confessed to the murder. The Leicester police should have been delighted, but there were some awkward questions hanging over the case. Fortunately, the new technique called **DNA** fingerprinting came to the rescue.

Making a DNA fingerprint

Body **cells** in flakes of skin, fingernails, hair, and body fluids (such as blood and saliva) all contain DNA—a complex code of chemicals in long molecular strands that are different and special for each individual. DNA can be used to identify a suspect by using an elaborate **procedure** known as **genetic** fingerprinting.

Genetic fingerprinting involves the following steps:

- A sample of DNA is taken from a suspect.

- A chemical called a "restriction enzyme" is added to the DNA. This chemical cuts it at specific places along the molecular strands.

- The pieces of DNA are added to a gel in a metal tray. An electric current is passed through the tray.

- The electric current causes the mixed-up DNA fragments to arrange themselves in order of size.

- A nylon sheet is placed over the DNA. The fragments attach themselves to it.

- A **radioactive** dye is added to the DNA.

- **X-ray** film is placed over the nylon sheet.

- X-ray film shows radioactivity, so the pattern made by the DNA can easily be seen.

- The film is developed and shows a distinct and unique pattern of DNA for each individual tested.

A forensic scientist examines two DNA "fingerprints."

Further investigation

The main problem with this case was that a body-fluid sample taken from the boy did not match those found on the bodies of the two girls. The boy's father was convinced his mentally challenged son was innocent. The father stated that his son had discovered Dawn Ashworth's body before the police, and was simply enjoying the attention he was getting as the supposed murderer. This boy's father suggested the police try out a new scientific breakthrough he had recently read about, made at nearby Leicester University. There, Dr. Alec Jeffreys had developed a technique to enable **forensic** scientists to compare **DNA** from body-fluid samples in the same way police compare fingerprints. Dr. Jeffreys was called in to help. Not only did he prove that the boy was not the murderer, he also confirmed that the same man had killed both girls.

Out to trap the culprit

In early 1987, Leicestershire Police ordered blood and saliva samples to be taken from every local male between the ages of 16 and 34. When no match was found, police officers traveled the country. They took samples from men who had lived in the area when the murders occurred, and had since moved away. But this massively expensive and **intricate** operation yielded no result. The murderer, it seemed, had got away.

Careless talk saves lives

It was a lunchtime bar conversation that finally gave the game away. Workers from a local bakery were gossiping about a colleague, Colin Pitchfork. One of them, Ian Kelly, admitted that Pitchfork had persuaded him to provide a fluid sample for the police on his behalf. Pitchfork told Kelly he had already given a sample under a different name to help out a friend. He was also afraid that because of his past criminal record the police would try to frame him for the murders. One of the bakery workers was deeply troubled by this conversation and eventually she told the police. Pitchfork was arrested soon after. A blood sample taken from him matched DNA evidence at the scenes of the two murders. He was sentenced to life imprisonment in 1988

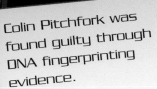

Colin Pitchfork was found guilty through DNA fingerprinting evidence.

Latest developments

DNA testing has progressed considerably since the 1980s. While Dr. Alec Jeffrey's method requires long, undamaged strands of DNA, forensic scientists today have developed new **procedures** that require far less **genetic** material. One technique, called mDNA screening, only requires DNA from the mitochondria—tiny parts of a body **cell** that make the energy it needs to work. The most recent technique, called SNP (single nucleotide polymorphism) identification, allows near-certain identification from only the tiniest amount of DNA.

These new techniques were used to provide positive identification of the 2,795 people thought to have died at the World Trade Center in New York City, on September 11, 2001. Only 287 whole bodies were found in the wreckage. Identification by standard means for the remaining victims has proved extremely difficult.

The *Maid of the Seas*

In the 30 years Boeing 747 "Jumbo" jets have been in service, they have carried millions of passengers. Only a very small number of passengers have died on such flights. Among them are the 259 passengers and crew of Pan Am flight 103, on a journey scheduled to take the 747 *Maid of the Seas* from Frankfurt via London to New York and Detroit. As passengers settled down for the overnight transatlantic flight, their cozy world was literally ripped apart. An explosion in the forward cargo hold punched a hole the size of a dinner plate in the side of the plane's thin metal body. They were 31,000 feet (9,500 meters) above the Scottish town of Lockerbie, close to the English border. The time was 7:03 P.M. on December 21, 1988.

Fatal dive

As the plane plowed through the freezing winter night at more than 550 miles per hour (885 kilometers per hour), the force of air tearing against the hole rapidly peeled back the aircraft's outer skin. Fatally weakened, the nose section broke away, and the rest of the plane went into a vertical dive before breaking up in the air. Back in London, where the plane had taken off barely half an hour before, air-traffic controllers monitoring the progress of Flight 103 were alarmed to see the blip on their radar screens rapidly lose height, then fade into several smaller blips.

The cockpit section of the *Maid of the Seas* lies in a field close to Lockerbie.

Villagers' horror

If the explosion had occurred a mere two or three seconds earlier or later, the villagers of Lockerbie would have escaped the horror visited upon them. In this thinly populated corner of Scotland they were unfortunate enough to be the destination of most of the 747's fractured body. An entire engine crashed on to the town, making a crater 15 feet (4.5 meters) deep. A wing full of fuel landed on one street, exploding with such intensity that it destroyed three houses and the eleven people inside them. But Lockerbie also saw some amazing escapes. One whole section of the **fuselage,** containing 60 passengers, landed in the middle of a street with houses on either side. Although 21 houses in all were demolished, only 11 residents died, out of the town's 1,500 inhabitants. Everyone on the plane was killed.

This aerial view of Lockerbie shows some of the destruction caused by the *Maid of the Seas.*

Crash causes

When news of the Lockerbie crash broke, all sorts of reasons for the crash were put forward: bad weather, pilot error, a bird flying into one of the huge jet engines—all were possibilities. Metal fatigue, metal parts of a plane crumbling or breaking due to age, was another potential cause.

But right from the start, the chief possibility was a bomb planted by a terrorist group or nation hostile to the United States. Libya was a prime suspect. Its leader, Colonel Gadhafi, had been attacked by U.S. jet fighters less than two years previously. Iran was also a suspect, because the U.S. Navy vessel USS *Vincennes* had recently accidentally destroyed an Iranian airliner with a surface-to-air missile.

After the crash

Rescue services were at the scene within minutes, and **investigators** followed in a matter of hours. At first light on a grim winter dawn, they were confronted with the full horror of the disaster. Bodies littered the town and surrounding fields, and large chunks of aircraft, including a half-intact cockpit section, lay strewn around. A Jumbo is made up of more than six million separate parts. Although most of the parts had landed around Lockerbie, there was an area of debris stretching over almost 1,000 square miles (2,500 square kilometers) of Scotland and northern England. It was the investigators' job to locate as much of the aircraft as possible.

Jigsaw puzzle

The larger pieces of the plane were taken away on flatbed trucks, and then investigators set about finding the rest. Over the next few months 1,000 volunteers scoured the area on hands and knees, picking up everything from drink carts and **fuselage** nuts and bolts, to the remains of passenger luggage. More than 90 percent of the 747 was recovered. Gradually, like a jigsaw puzzle, the massive 300-ton aircraft was laid out in a vast hangar. Piece by piece the plane and its contents took on its strange exploded shape, now recognizable as it once had been, but horribly different. Each piece that came in, no matter how big or small, was **X-rayed** and subjected to chemical tests and microscopic examination.

The *Maid of the Seas* is shown being pieced together during the crash investigation.

Turning up clues

This **intricate** task revealed vital clues, and allowed investigators to offer substantial proof that the crash had been caused by a bomb. Luggage, a luggage container, and remains of the front baggage compartment all showed **evidence** of some sort of explosion that had blown material outward with great force.

Fragments from the explosion had embedded themselves in these items, and this showed up under **electron-microscope** examination. Such examination also revealed a noticeable change in the structure of the metal skin of the plane's body close to the blast. This corresponded to previously recorded information on changes in metal structure following exposure to explosion.

Furthermore, tests with **gas chromatography** revealed the presence in the forward baggage compartment of two chemicals known as PETN and RDX. They are both major ingredients in the high explosive Semtex. **Forensic** results such as these were enough to convince investigators that they were dealing with a case of mass murder, rather than an accident.

Gas chromatography

One of a forensic investigator's most useful tools is the gas chromatograph. It is a device that burns a small sample of a suspicious substance with gas, and then analyzes the gases that are given off when it is burned. These gases pass through a detector that sends **data** to a computer, which in turn identifies the substance.

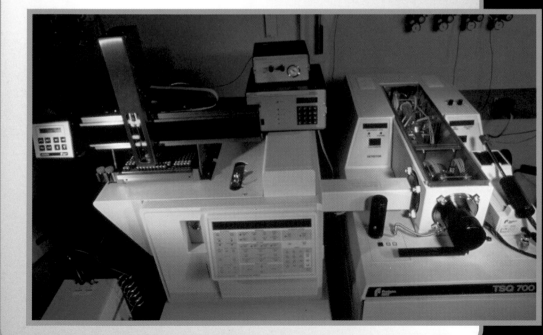

Causes and culprits

Most **investigators** accepted the cause of the crash, although a handful remain unconvinced by the bomb theory. Some still thought the disaster could have been an accident. After all, passenger planes have occasionally fallen inexplicably from the sky. Three years before the Lockerbie disaster, for example, a Japanese Boeing 747 (the same kind of aircraft as the one flying Flight 103), crashed near Tokyo, killing all 520 passengers and crew.

A U.S. government spokesperson shows journalists the kind of radio-cassette player used to hide the bomb.

Next came the question of who planted the bomb. By piecing together the luggage and luggage containers, investigators traced the explosion to a bomb inside a Toshiba radio cassette player called the "Bombeat." Fragments showed the radio had been hidden in a brown suitcase.

Further **investigation** showed this suitcase had been purchased and packed in Malta. It had then been placed on the plane by a Libyan passenger who failed to board the plane. Eventually in 2000, two Libyans were brought to trial, and sent to prison. The case was very controversial, and several highly respected lawyers have claimed that the **evidence** against the men was faulty.

Some good news

The Lockerbie tragedy led to changes in airline **procedures.** Now, if a passenger checks in luggage but does not board the plane, the luggage is removed. Sophisticated explosive detection devices have also been developed that make smuggling deadly packages aboard planes much more difficult.

Youssef Shaaban stands trial for the Lockerbie bombing.

But, although most people accept that a bomb destroyed the *Maid of the Seas*, there is still a great deal of unease about the two men convicted of planting it. As Jane Swire, the mother of 23-year-old victim Flora Swire, puts it: "We would like to know before we die the background and the reason and who did this terrible crime." So far, Mrs. Swire can be pretty certain of why Flight 103 crashed. But she, and many others from the victims' families, is not convinced the right men are being punished.

Evidence for a bomb on Flight 103

Conclusions are rarely based on just one piece of evidence. There are several reasons to suspect that a bomb was planted aboard the *Maid of the Seas*:

- Chemical presence—detected via **gas chromatography**—of the high explosive Semtex.

- **Electron microscope** examination revealed both structural changes to the aircraft normally indicating explosive damage, and the presence of embedded fragments from the explosion.

- Fragments found of **detonators** used in terrorist bomb-making.

- A loud bang heard on the aircraft cockpit voice recording just before the crash.

- No evidence to support the theory that metal fatigue, or any other accidental occurrence, caused the crash.

FILE CLOSED

33

"Omar killed me"

Life was extremely comfortable for wealthy widow Ghislaine Marchal. She lived in a luxury villa in the town of Mougins on the French Riviera. While her gardener, a perfectly pleasant and mild-mannered Moroccan man named Omar Raddad, busied himself in the villa grounds, she would sit in the sun doing a crossword puzzle or two. A sharp and intelligent woman, Madame Marchal always finished them in impressively short time. But in the summer of 1991, something hideous happened to her.

Written in blood

On the evening of June 24, neighbors discovered Madame Marchal's stabbed and beaten body in the cellar of the villa. Just above where she lay, the words *"Omar m'a tuer"* ("Omar has killed me") were written in her own blood on the wall. The message was written again as "Omar m'a T." Raddad was immediately arrested. At his trial **graphologists** testified that they were "more than 60 percent certain" the handwriting was Madame Marchal's. This was good enough for the judge, and Raddad was sentenced to eighteen years in prison. The fact that he had gambling debts, and 4,000 francs had been stolen from the villa, seemed to offer a firm **motive** for the killing.

Omar Raddad (center) shortly after his arrest for the murder of Ghislaine Marchal.

A fair cop?

On the surface, the case seemed obvious enough. But it has since become one of France's most talked-about murders. There are several reasons to suspect that the French police had not caught the right man.

First, the bloody message contained a basic grammatical mistake. "*Tuer*" means "to kill" rather than "killed." Few people who knew the well-educated Madame Marchal could imagine her making such an elementary mistake— even if she did write the message as she lay dying.

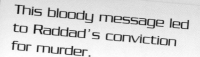

This bloody message led to Raddad's conviction for murder.

Written evidence

Graphology is the study of handwriting. Some aspects of graphology are more scientific than others. Comparing handwriting with known and questioned scripts is a common **forensic procedure.** Many legal cases have hinged on whether handwriting, typewriter and printer text, or even rubber stamps are genuine or forged to resemble those of a specific person.

One aspect of graphology open to question concerns handwriting and personality. Everyone has distinctive handwriting, and some graphologists claim that this enables an expert to deduce aspects of that person's personality. The way letters are formed, how they join to other letters, how much writing slants, how big or small it is, and the spaces between words, lines, and letters are all said to indicate specific personality traits. In terms of winning the respect of scientists, this lies somewhere between the objective certainties of chemical **analysis,** and the superstitions of astrology. While some graphologists have made remarkable and correct assumptions about people's personalities based on handwriting samples, many scientists remain unconvinced.

Fresh evidence

Raddad always protested his innocence with great sincerity, and gradually he began to attract some high-profile supporters, including French president Jacques Chirac and Moroccan King Hassan II. Fresh **evidence** then came to light. Other graphology experts were called upon and they reported that "it was not possible to attribute with certainty" who had written the fateful bloodstained words. Even more importantly, further **forensic** tests on the blood used to form the letters revealed two different sources of blood, one of which was male. This blood was not Raddad's. Finally, re-examined **autopsy** evidence revealed that it was more likely that Marchal died on the day she was found, January 24, when Raddad was visiting friends, rather than the previous estimate—on January 23—when the gardener had spent all day working at the house.

Out of prison

So, in 1998, four years into his sentence, Raddad was released, following a pardon by the French president. Having been all too eager to arrest him, the police now had to search for a new killer. One theory suggested that relatives eager to get their hands on Madame Marchal's wealth had had her killed by a Swiss hit man, who then tried to place the blame on Raddad. Further **investigations** have now been hampered by poor collection and storage of evidence at the scene of the crime. Fingerprints were not taken, evidence was later destroyed, and the weapons used in the murder (a knife and some other kind of blunt object) were never found. A further autopsy is out of the question because Madame Marchal was cremated. But one major mystery still remains: the cellar had no windows and the door was blocked from the inside by an iron bed frame. If Marchal's murderer had written the words incriminating Omar Raddad, how did he get out of the cellar? To this day, nobody knows.

Bloody clues

Blood is almost always present at a murder scene. It offers forensic **investigators** a prime source of evidence. For this reason, a blood-test kit is almost always carried to the scene of the crime.

Bloodstains may reveal fingerprints or footprints, and any blood shed by the murderer in a struggle may serve to identify him or her through **DNA** evidence, blood group, or other biological indicators. There are four main blood groups (A, B, AB, and O) with several recognizable subsections within each group.

Bloodstains fall into five major patterns: drops, splashes, spurts, smears, and trails. By locating and noting such patterns, investigators can recreate what happened during a murder.

A forensic scientist takes a blood sample from a murder weapon.

The Washington, D.C., Snipers

The killing spree left police **investigators** baffled. On October 2, 2002, a series of **random sniper** slayings around the Washington, D.C., area began. By October 7, six people had been killed and two seriously injured. There were no **witnesses** to any of the shootings, and no link in age, race, or gender between the victims. Only the bullet used, a .223-**caliber** rifle round, indicated that the murderer was the same in all cases. Since each of the six victims was killed with a single shot from some distance, it was also thought the killer was probably a man—maybe even an ex-soldier. "Most people kill for what they think are good reasons, so random killings are simply very, very difficult to solve," Carl Klockars, Professor of Criminal Justice and Sociology at the University of Delaware, told newspaper journalists.

Lines of police officers search for bullets or cartridges at the scene of a sniper attack.

Card clue

All through October the killings continued. During a three-week period there were thirteen victims. There was no rhyme or reason to the incidents. Whoever was doing this enjoyed playing with people's lives. They admitted it, too. At the scene of one shooting, a tarot (fortune-telling) card was left with the chilling words "Mister Policeman, I am God" written on it.

Unexpected help

Police were baffled, but help came from unexpected places. Cases like these always attract crank phone calls to the authorities from people claiming to be the murderer. But one persistent caller seemed to know some facts about the killings that had not been released to the press. Frustrated by the police's reluctance to believe he was the sniper, the caller demanded to be taken seriously, and angrily told the police to "check with the people of Montgomery." They did. Inquiries to police authorities in Montgomery, Alabama, revealed that a recent liquor store robbery had left one woman dead and another badly injured. The killer had dropped a scrap of paper with a fingerprint on it. Maybe the robber and the sniper were one and the same person?

Random killings

Nothing in the choice of victims or location of the shootings gave anything away to the police.

October 2:   man, 55, shot dead in parking lot Wheaton, Maryland

October 3:   man, 39
man, 54
woman, 34
woman, 25 all shot dead in street, Maryland
woman, 72, shot dead at bus stop, Washington, D.C.

October 4:   woman, 43, wounded in parking lot

October 7:   boy, 13, wounded in school playground, Maryland

October 9:   man, 53, shot dead at gas station, Virginia

October 11:   man, shot dead at gas station, Virginia

October 14:   woman, 47, shot dead at store, Virginia

October 19:   man, 37, injured in street, Virginia

October 22:   man shot at bus stop, Maryland

Another lead

Meanwhile, Washington police were following up another line of **investigation.** One resident in Tacoma, Washington, had remembered two very odd neighbors—a Gulf War veteran named John Allen Muhammad, who was 41 years old, and a 17-year-old Jamaican boy named John Lee Malvo. The two were said to have a "sergeant-recruit"-type relationship, and would often use a tree trunk in their backyard for target practice. The suspicious caller to the Washington police had a strong Jamaican accent. The tarot card contained the phrase "Mister Policeman"—a characteristic Jamaican expression. Furthermore, a letter to the police, also thought to come from the **sniper,** had phrases in it that were recognizably Jamaican. It was all beginning to come together.

House call

On Wednesday October 23, the police swooped on the house in Tacoma. Although Muhammad and Malvo were gone, a fingerprint match to the liquor store robbery was found. There was another lead as well. Muhammad had a 1990 Chevrolet Caprice, license plate number NDA-21Z, registered under his name. On Thursday, October 24, Washington, D.C., police chief Charles Moose made a dramatic midnight television appeal for anyone seeing the car to immediately call the police. A photograph of Muhammad had also been unearthed, and was shown on television.

Police search the Tacoma residence of Muhammad and Malvo.

Snatch squad

With the car identified and a mug shot in circulation, time quickly ran out for the Washington, D.C., area killers. Within an hour of the television appeal, a motorist called police on his cell phone to report he was in the same rest stop as the Chevrolet, and that two people were asleep inside. John Allen Muhammad and John Lee Malvo woke to the sound of helicopter blades swishing above them, and looked out of their car windows to see a squad of police officers surrounding them. As the two were led away, the car was searched. A sniper scope (a special kind of sighting attachment for a sniper rifle), a tripod, and a .223-**caliber** rifle were found in the trunk.

This is John Lee Malvo shortly after his arrest.

Bad leads

Cases such as this always produce a huge response from the public. The police have an extremely difficult job sifting useful and useless leads. During most of the murder investigation they thought that the killer or killers were operating from a white van, as witnesses sometimes reported one at the scene of a shooting. This information was released to the public, and while the killers were at large, the sight of a white van in any location usually sent pedestrians scurrying away. It turned out to be a completely false lead. White vans are common vehicles, and their presence at some of the shootings was pure coincidence.

Solve It!

In the dead of night a shadowy figure creeps up to a closed first-floor window, carelessly trampling the flowers that lie in a neatly arranged display around the low apartment building wall. With a well-practiced gloved hand, the man slips a screwdriver into the bottom of the window frame, and begins to push the window up. Slowly, slowly, it rises up in its frame. The **intruder** laughs quietly to himself. He cannot believe how easy it is to break into this residence.

The bungled burglary

When the window is open enough for him to get through, the intruder peers inside. That night there is a new moon, and he can see nothing of the black interior. He parts the curtains and ducks down through the window, gingerly placing one foot, then the other, on the inside floor.

Suddenly, the intruder is knocked to his feet, and finds himself fending off heavy blows to his head. He realized in an instant he has climbed into the apartment owner's bedroom, rather than his living room. Instinctively, he lashes out with the screwdriver that he still holds in his hand. Contact is made. His assailant gives a startled cry, and falls over.

Fingerprint identification is still one of a **forensic** investigator's chief weapons.

```
- (F1)  Candidat : HIT
  (F2)  Candidat : NO_HIT
  (F3)  Sans decision : NUL
  (F4)  Doigt suivant
```

The intruder stands above his victim, and reaches into his leather jacket for a pistol equipped with a silencer. Quickly he fires two shots into the body, and **cartridge cases** clatter on the wood floor as they are ejected from the gun.

An eerie stillness follows, and the intruder becomes aware of a sharp pain on top of his head. He places a gloved hand to the injury and is aware that he is bleeding. He needs to escape as quickly as possible. He looks for the door. There must be a switch. He clicks it on. In the harsh light he notices that his glove is covered with blood. There on the door is a jacket. He quickly rifles through the pockets, seizing a wallet. His hands are shaking, and he fumbles with the wallet. In frustration he removes a glove and takes out the wallet's contents—$200. He puts the glove back on, pockets the money, throws the wallet on the floor, then switches off the light to make a hasty exit back through the window.

Outside, the world is still and quiet. No one knows what has happened. He looks around, and then vanishes into the shadows. Three days later the intruder is arrested at his home. Police leave his residence carrying a pistol with silencer attachment in a sealed plastic bag.

How many clues did the intruder leave at the scene of the crime?

Glossary

analysis detailed examination of something in order to understand it better

assault aggressive physical attack on someone, intending to cause harm

autopsy examination of a body to discover the cause of death

ballistics science of bullets, also known as projectiles, and firearms

caliber width of a gun barrel, and the bullets that will fit into such a gun barrel

cartilage tough, elastic tissue found in the nose, ear, throat, and other parts of the body

cartridge case part of a projectile containing the explosives that fire the bullet from a gun. After firing, the cartridge case is ejected from the weapon.

cell smallest independent unit in an organism

Communist supports communism, a political system in which the state controls the wealth and industry of a country

data observations, measurements, or facts used in an investigation

database information stored on a computer

detonator part of a bomb that sets off the explosion

dissected cut open for detailed examination

DNA type of molecule in the form of a twisted double strand (known as a double helix) found in every cell of every living thing. It is a major component of chromosomes (the rod-shaped structures in a cell nucleus) and carries genetic information (the information that determines an organism's characteristics).

DNA sample small amount of DNA

electron negatively charged particle that orbits the nucleus of an atom

electron microscope microscope that uses electron beams instead of visible light to magnify an object so it can be seen in amazing detail

evidence something that is used to prove that a crime has been committed, or a specific person has committed that crime

forensics use of science and medicine to solve crime

fuselage body of an aircraft

gas chromatography identifies substances by burning a sample with gas and then analyzing the gases it gives off

genetic concerned with genes, the basic units consisting of a sequence of DNA that transmits characteristics from one generation to the next

glass plate negatives
photographic technique used in
the 19th and early 20th century
where a negative image suitable
to make photographic prints is
created on a plate of glass,
rather than a plastic film

graphologist someone who
studies handwriting

guerrilla member of an irregular
fighting force, usually one that is
rebelling against a government

intricate something that is
detailed and complicated

intruder someone who is in a
situation or place where they are
not wanted, or should not be

investigation formal inquiry to
find out as much information as
possible about something

investigator someone who
investigates

lens curved glass, which when
looked through, makes an
object appear bigger

light microscope microscope
that uses lenses and natural light
to examine objects in much
greater detail

massacre many people being
killed at one time

mortuary special building in a
hospital or police station, where
dead bodies are kept

motive reason for doing
something

pathologist doctor who
specializes in a branch of
medicine concerned with the
study of disease, or any other
abnormal changes to the body
that have occurred at death

procedure particular way of
doing something

radioactive used to describe a
substance that gives off energy in
the form of a stream of particles,
owing to the decaying of its
unstable atoms

random something that happens
by chance, or an action that has
no prior plan

regime particular government

ricin poison obtained from castor
oil beans that can cause major
health problems and death

sniper someone who fires a
weapon, usually a rifle, from a
concealed position at an
unsuspecting victim

specimen sample of a particular
substance for analysis

suicide killing oneself
intentionally

two-way transfer basis of
forensic investigation that every
contact leaves a trace

witness someone who sees
something happen. Witnesses are
often used in a court of law to
give evidence at a trial.

X-ray high-energy
electromagnetic radiation with
a wavelength that is capable
of penetrating solid objects

Get into Forensics

Forensics is a complex and fascinating business. Investigators may be called upon to make identifications from DNA fragments, take fingerprints from a crime scene, check photographs for fakes, examine paper fibers under an electron microscope, find the age of ancient bones using radiocarbon dating, match tire tracks left by a getaway car, or compare known dental records to the corpse of an unknown person.

One person alone cannot master such a wide range of skills, and those involved in forensic investigations often perform highly specialized tasks. Ballistics experts, for example, will match projectiles with weapons and detect traces of explosives on fabric or skin. Toxicologists may be called on by a pathologist carrying out an autopsy to examine a particular organ for indications of a hard-to-detect poison.

In their way of working, all forensic investigators are scientific or medical professionals. In fact, the range of skills required is so broad it covers almost every aspect of science and medicine: physics, chemistry, biology, medicine and dentistry, anthropology, archaeology, and psychology. So any reader wanting to pursue a career in forensics will need to begin with an interest in science.

Useful Websites

A website that gives details of the criminal mind and the methods they use:
    http://www.crimelibrary.com/index.html

A site that gives detailed articles about various crime scene investigator techniques and tools:
    http://www.crime-scene-investigator.net/

The FBI's website for young adults:
    http://www.fbi.gov/kids/6th12th/6th12th.htm

A site dedicated to finding the killers in unsolved cases:
    http://www.unsolvedcrimes.com/

Further Reading

Binns, Tristan Boyer. *The FBI: Federal Bureau of Investigation.* Chicago: Heinemann Library, 2003.

Jackson, Donna M. *The Bone Detectives: How Forensic Anthropologists Solve Crimes and Uncover Mysteries of the Dead.* New York: Little Brown & Company, 2001.

McIntosh, Neil. *Cybercrime.* Chicago: Raintree, 2003.

Pentland, Peter and Pennie Stoyles. *Forensic Science.* Broomall, Penn.: Chelsea House, 2003.

Woodford, Chris. *Criminal Investigations.* Chicago: Raintree, 2001.

Woolf, Alex. *Investigating Thefts & Heists.* Chicago: Heinemann Library, 2004.

FORENSIC FILES

Index